# THE ILLUSTRATED HISTORY OF

# SEDDON

# ATKINSON

## TRUCKS & BUSES

# THE ILLUSTRATED HISTORY OF
# SEDDON
# ATKINSON
## TRUCKS & BUSES

## NICK BALDWIN

A **FOULIS** Motoring Book

First published 1990

Published by:
**Haynes Publishing Group**
Sparkford, Nr Yeovil, Somerset. BA22 7JJ.
England

**Haynes Publications Inc.**
861 Lawrence Drive, Newbury Park,
California 91320 USA

**British Library Cataloguing in
Publication Data**
Baldwin, Nick
    The illustrated history of
    Seddon-Atkinson trucks and buses.
    1. Commercial vehicles
    I. Title
    629.2'24
    ISBN 0-85429-706-5

**Library of Congress Catalog Card
Number**
89-85903

Editor: Rob Iles

Typeset in Rockwell med rom 12/13pt
and printed in England by J. H. Haynes &
Co Ltd.

# Introduction and Acknowledgements

Seddon and Atkinson carved a very special niche for themselves in different spheres of the diesel market. Atkinson's history went right back to steam days but the firm did not become a major maker of heavy vehicles until the 1940s, at much the same time that Seddon was tapping demand for a cheap and lightweight diesel vehicle to compete with contemporary mass-produced petrol rivals. In the 1950s and 60s both firms went through a fascinating era of "specials" manufacture and in many ways were the ideal partners when they merged in 1970. The subsequent story of international finance and takeovers seems out of keeping with the traditional and down to earth Lancastrian qualities of the two firms.

The fact that they came through the International Harvester debacle virtually unscathed says a lot for the quiet determination of the firm's employees and the loyal backing of their customers. Under the new regime of ENASA, Seddon Atkinson seemed to be once again on the road to international success with a sophisticated range using the best components from many sources.

To many people the vast number of different shapes and sizes of vehicle depicted in this book will come as something of a surprise. I make no apologies for showing a disproportionate number of custom-built trucks, simply because these are less familiar than the famous standard models, which, however, are shown in a great many forms. The firms have always fascinated me, not least because in my only two forays on to the Stock Market, Seddon came up trumps and made up for all my losses on Guy!

Thanks are due to everyone who helped with pictures. This includes the late Prince Marshall of *Old Motor* fame, Frank Whalley at Seddon Atkinson, Niels Jansen, Alan B. Cross, Nick Georgano, Peter Bevan (formerly of Halls of Finchley), Malcolm Dungworth and the Commercial Vehicle and Road Transport Club of 8 Tackbrook Road, Uxbridge, Middlesex, UB8 2QS.

Edward, Harry, Samuel and Steven were the sons of Samuel Atkinson, an engineer who travelled the world installing looms for making cloth. The sons went into the cotton industry in their early teens. At the age of 14 Edward, born in 1875, transferred to Coulthards, later to make steam wagons and merge with the Spurrier family firm in Leyland to create Leyland Motors Ltd. Edward joined a firm in Preston that made petrol engined front wheel attachments for previously horsedrawn vehicles. Then in 1907 some of the brothers started Atkinson & Co. as millwrights and general engineers at Frenchwood Avenue, in Preston, variously described as the home of Samuel Birch Atkinson and a partner in the firm, George Hunt.

The firm soon specialised in vehicle repairs and maintenance in Kendal Street, Preston, where a few petrol engined vans were reputedly built in around 1910. The firm also held an agency for the Sentinel steam wagon, then made in Glasgow. With the transfer of its production to Shrewsbury Atkinson lost the agency and in 1916 decided to build its own steamers based on its knowledge of Sentinels, and strongly resembling them. Shown here is a 1920 advertisement for the new wagon and a contemporary Sentinel by way of contrast.

A five-acre site was bought nearby and production started there in 1918, the Kendal Street premises being retained for repairs. Over a hundred men were employed in 1919 and 150 by 1922, when up to three wagons per week were built. These employed the American invented double-acting Uniflow type of twin-cylinder engine. The steam from the vertical cross water tube boiler was admitted to the cylinders via ball valves at one end and exhausted through ports in the other end of the cylinders. Plenty of torque made the fitment of a gearbox unnecessary, though some had two-speed epicyclic gearing. One such worked in the hilly Lake District with a trailer and combined load of twelve tons of slates. From 1923 an articulated twelve-tonner was offered, as well as a diminutive 2½ ton "run about".

Shown here are general arrangement drawings plus a photograph of a six-tonner during assembly.

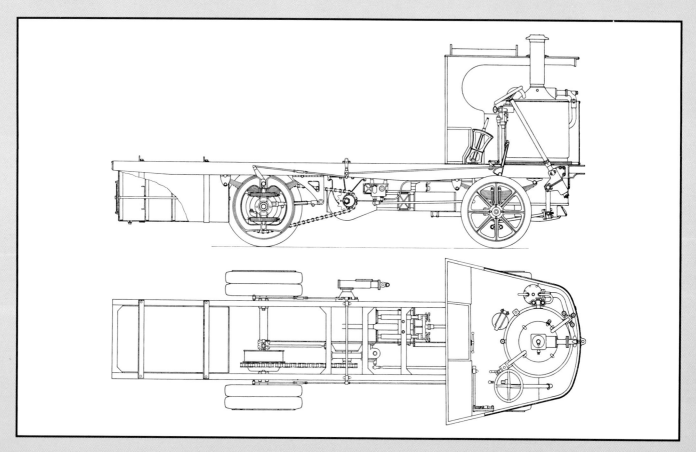

*Photographs on this page and overleaf:*

Atkinson had a blinkered view of steam and did not see the writing on the wall even when sales began to slow down in the mid 1920s and when first Leyland sold its steam remnants to Atkinson in 1926, followed by Mann selling theirs to Atkinson in 1929.

There seem to have been various family rivalries at the time and the firm was undoubtedly in difficulties when Edward Atkinson decided to seek help from mine engineers and Pagefield lorry makers, Walker Bros. of Wigan. Major James Scarlet Ashcroft Walker took up £3,000 worth of preference shares in 1925 and the firm was renamed Atkinson Walker Wagons Ltd. In exchange Walker Brothers were to make the Uniflow engines in their steam winch department but very few orders were forthcoming. Edward Atkinson had cancer and was unable to pay any dividends on the preference shares and finally abandoned wagon production in 1929 after a grand total of about 325 Atkinsons had been built. (545 is a figure also quoted, though this presupposes that all chassis numbers were allocated, which was probably not the case.) The final years were made possible by Walker's money and by a cancellation fee from Manchester Co-op Society which had ordered a hundred waggons.

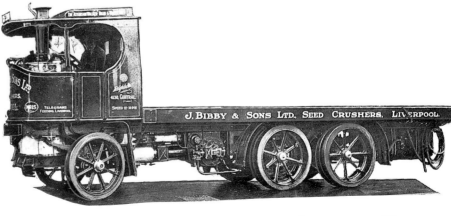

Shown here is a 1928 Atkinson-Walker advertisement and an assortment of steamers. The tractor was one of a type that served in Liverpool up to the 1950s, thanks to the acquisition of the remaining spares by Bibbys in the early 1930s. Note the rear bogie spread in the advertisement compared with the production reality on the Bibby six--wheeler and also the drawbar trailer, a business that was to be the salvation of the Atkinson company.

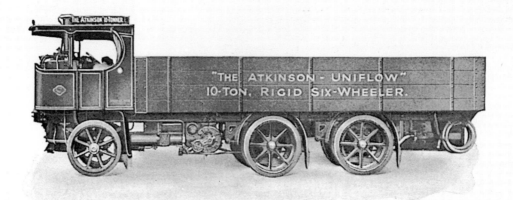

The one happy outcome of the liaison between Walker and Pagefield was that the former converted one of the latter's steam railcars in Ireland to diesel traction and built up a thriving railway business on the strength of its success. Gardner diesels were used and in 1930 one was installed in a Pagefield lorry, making it the first manufactured in Britain to be offered as a complete entity as opposed to a conversion. Shown here is a petrol powered Pagefield used in the Pagefield System of demountable refuse trailers towed between houses by horse and then whisked to the dump by lorry. The System was made much cheaper to run when Gardner powered. Atkinson was soon to learn from Pagefield's experience.

This is the only known surviving Atkinson steamer. It was built by Tom Varley and friends from parts recovered from Australia in 1976. It had been exported there in 1918 and worked for 28 years before being abandoned at a derelict gold mine in the bush.

The Atkinson factory closed with the end of the steamers though a dozen men employed by the firm's receivers continued repairing and servicing wagons and converting lorries into six-wheelers at Kendal Street, Preston and building trailers. Edward Atkinson died in January 1932 and a year later the firm he had founded was acquired for £6,500 by London garage owner, W. G. Allen, whose father had started Nightingale Garage. Allen was chairman of Atkinson Lorries (1933) Ltd and H. B. Fielding was managing director. He had effectively run the firm since 1931 when the Bank had sold the business to three businessmen from St. Helens and remained in charge until his death in 1949.

*Photograph on opposite page:*
Atkinson Lorries (1933) Ltd. was still primarily a commercial vehicle garage, though a few internal combustion engined vehicles had been built, using parts of other vehicles and proprietary engines, since 1931. Most efforts centred round trailers, conversions of four-wheel lorries to balance beam six-wheelers, the uprating of braking systems and the replacement of solid tyred wheels with pneumatics. Ernest Philbrow and then Frank Thomas designed complete new chassis and these entered limited production at a new factory in Marsh Lane, Preston, in 1934. However, before that came three diesel Atkinsons made mostly of new components. The 12 ton capacity six-wheeler dated from late 1931 and had a Blackstone BMV6 diesel. The four-wheeler was a 1932 vehicle with Dorman 4RBL diesel and there was also another with forward control mysteriously built for the Italian Ministry of War.

*Photographs overleaf:*
Following the Pagefield connection already mentioned and the chance meeting of an Atkinson representative with the driver of an elderly Albion fitted with one of the new Gardner LW engines, which started easily on a cold morning, this make of engine was standardised. Other regular Atkinson features were Kirkstall axles, Hardy Spicer propshafts and David Brown four- or five-speed gearboxes. Production centred around seven-ton four-wheelers, ten- and twelve-ton six-wheelers, and from 1937 ten-ton Chinese six-wheelers and fifteen-ton eight-wheelers.

The two four-wheelers without the circular A motif date from 1935. The Argyll Transport seven-tonner had a 5LW engine and carried sheep, whilst Stewart & Hill's lorry had a moving floor. James Pickup's tipper dates from 1936 and the 1937 six-wheelers flank a 1936 Leyland Hippo.

Meanwhile over in Salford, Lancashire, a transport business and garage founded in 1919 by Thomas, Robert and Herbert Seddon and Ernest Foster, was flourishing. It had run Commer charabancs and obtained an agency for the make, followed by one for Lancia in 1925. Harry Redmond became the firm's auditor in 1926 and soon joined as company secretary. In 1929 Foster and Seddon began reconditioning popular types of lorry, particularly Leylands, and in 1932 obtained an agency for Reo vehicles. These were of American origin, though assembled in London. Reo Speed Wagons had a good reputation for performance and competitive pricing, though as can be seen in this photograph, a poor ratio of payload space to overall length!

Robert Seddon had been thinking of designing a lorry since the 1920s and new legislation permitting 30 mph instead of 20 mph operation by goods vehicles with an unladen weight of under $2^1/_2$ tons gave him the impetus he required. Launched in late 1938 the Foster and

Seddon, or Seddon as it soon became, could carry a remarkable six tons and was the first to use the Perkins six-cylinder diesel as original equipment. It was by far the most cost effective lorry of the era and about two hundred were built before war intervened – a remarkable figure especially as Atkinson only made about fifty of its expensive vehicles in the 1930s, including a few $2^1/_2$ ton ULW types in 1939 with Gardner 4LK engines. Most of Seddon's wartime efforts went into trailers for the Ministry of Supply.

Far from being held back by wartime problems, Atkinson really began to thrive. The Ministry of Supply in 1940 permitted only it and ERF to make six-wheelers for civilian purposes. The first order to Atkinson was for sixty 6LW powered six-wheelers. Then a year later one hundred more were ordered with AEC engines, AEC having greater engine building than chassis manufacturing capacity. Finally one hundred eight-wheelers with AEC engines were ordered.

Here we see six- and eight-wheel tankers working for the Pool (petrol) Board, and a flat bed six-wheeler, with, like all the others, wartime blackout masks and white-painted extremities to improve close-up visibility.

Component shortages after the War resulted in Atkinson building its own five-speed gearboxes. Otherwise the mix was much as before. A new chief engineer, J. J. Naylor, had joined the firm in 1942 and was to remain until 1956. The works manager from 1945 was Francis B. Caunt from Leyland, who became managing director on the death of H. B. Fielding. Over one hundred men were employed in 1948, when the firm became a Public Company. By then production had started at a new factory on a 4$\frac{1}{2}$ acre site at Winery Lane, Walton le Dale, near Preston, and the old Marsh Lane premises had become the service depot. Styling had changed very little, as the 1946 six-wheeler, 1950 four-wheeler (with Goddard alloy body) and 1951 eight-wheeler confirm.

*Photographs above and overleaf:*

Seddon Motors Ltd., as it was now called, was also prospering in the early post-war years. Its scattered factories in and around Salford were making eight chassis per week, and twelve to thirteen soon afterwards, and in 1948 all work was transferred to Woodstock Factory, the former Claudel Hobson aircraft carburettor plant at Shaw, near Oldham, which cost £300,000. An idea of the industrial surroundings of this district of Lancashire, with its dark satanic mills, is given in this evocative view of a six-tonner on test. The cattle truck dates from 1947, as does the Clark distribution van. The postwar six-tonner had a five-speed gearbox and stronger frame, springs and axles and was known as the Mk 5.

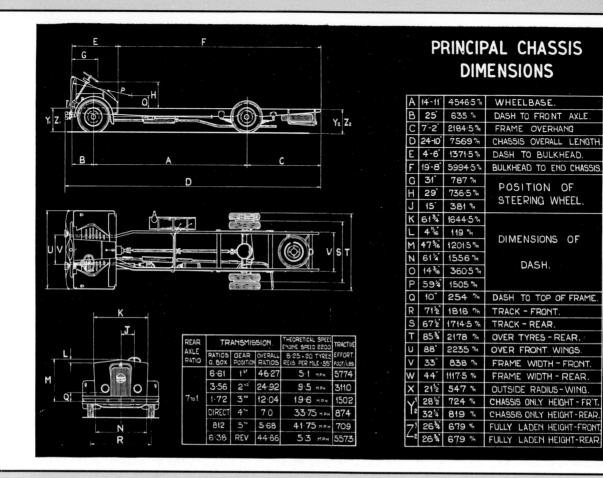

# The SEDDON in INDIA

Illustrations above show some of a fleet of 15 "SEDDON" Passenger Vehicles recently supplied to THE BOMBAY STATE TRANSPORT. Their ability to operate with equal facility in the heat of an Indian Summer or during the period of monsoon rains is a tribute to their all round efficiency.

## A REPEAT ORDER FOR 75 SIMILAR VEHICLES IS CONVINCING PROOF OF "SEDDON" QUALITY

Built on the "Seddon" Mk. 4 Chassis, designed for use as a General Service Bus or Luxury Coach, with either left or right hand drive, that meet all the requirements for use under the varying conditions affecting overseas operators.

*Illustrations on previous two pages and the photograph above:*

The bus version of the Mk 5 was the Mk 4 with lengthened chassis but the same mechanical components and Perkins engine (though a handful had Meadows petrol engines). A dimensional blueprint is shown here, along with a 1949 advertisement describing an Indian order. The Western National bus was photographed ahead of a Morris-Commercial van by Allan B. Cross in Taunton in 1952 and dates from late 1948. Bodywork on the Mk 4 was by numerous firms, an example being Thurgood, whose 1949 advertisement is shown. Seddon also built PSV and commercial bodywork at the adjoining Pennine Coach Craft plant, and by then employed 600 men. In 1959 Seddon needed more capital for expansion and became a public company under the title Seddon Diesel Vehicles Ltd. with R. H. Seddon as Chairman, H. Seddon and H. Redmond joint managing directors, and Sir Stanley Bell and H. Daley as directors. At least half of production went for export.

Atkinson built a few lighter models with Gardner 4LK engines for 18,480 lbs GVW. It also experimented with ways of modernising the appearance of the vehicle, as this stylish 1949 advertisement shows. However, the distinctive radiator was to remain an Atkinson feature for the next twenty-five years and is typified by the Tyburn tanker of 1954 with its Knight of the Road emblem. Compared with Seddon, Atkinson was still relatively small, as an output of 180 vehicles in 1948 testifies.

KNIGHT OF THE ROAD

ALP 49

Uncertainties over what would happen to Atkinson orders with the takeover of so many of its customers by BRS led to the firm trying to find ways of diversifying. Own account operators

were unaffected so Atkinson built some low loading van chassis for them with the outriggers actually built into the chassis, which therefore did not need a subframe. Ultra heavy duty tractors were built for South Africa from 1950 with Gardner 8LW engines. Another new departure was PSV chassis made possible by Atkinson's good relationship with Gardner, which ensured that the much sought-after horizontal HLW was available. The first chassis was shown at Earls Court in 1950 and here we see it outside the Winery Lane offices in 1951 ready for Sandown Tours of Burnley, with 6HLW, Atkinson five-speed gearbox and Kirkstall hypoid axle. Its PM746H chassis is also shown in diagrammatic form.

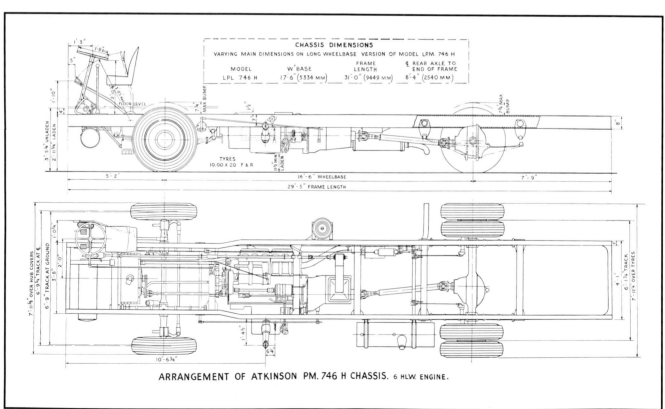

CHASSIS DIMENSIONS

VARYING MAIN DIMENSIONS ON LONG WHEELBASE VERSION OF MODEL L.P.M. 746 H

| MODEL | W'BASE | FRAME LENGTH | ℄ REAR AXLE TO END OF FRAME |
|---|---|---|---|
| LPL 746 H | 17'-6" (5334 MM) | 31'-0" (9449 MM) | 8'-4" (2540 MM) |

ARRANGEMENT OF ATKINSON PM. 746 H CHASSIS. 6 HLW. ENGINE.

*Photographs on the previous page and above:*

It seems extraordinary in retrospect but in those early postwar years Seddon had the mid weight semi-mass-produced market more or less to itself. Bedford and Ford had yet to offer diesel vehicles and of the firms that did, very few used competitively priced and robust Perkins units. Another relatively new truck maker, Jensen, was perhaps the most direct competitor, though firms like Guy also made lightweight trucks in this weight range. Others like AEC, Leyland and Thornycroft made their own engines and offered complete ranges, whilst Foden, ERF and Atkinson tended to concentrate on maximum weight high quality chassis.

Here we see a 1950 tanker with all-metal cab and a pair of contemporary vans. The builder of the Luton-type body is not known but Cunard was responsible for the other.

*Photographs on the opposite page and overleaf top:*

Exports were going well at Seddon and the Low Countries were avid buyers of Mk 5 lorries. In Holland they were sold by Van Twist from 1948 and in Belgium by Hocké, whose names appeared on the radiator badges. From 1954 some special municipal types based on Seddon chassis with Perkins engine, Moss gearbox and Kirkstall axles were sold, purely as Van Twist with forward control cabs resembling the contemporary DAF. As can be seen, even the more generally recognisable Seddons also had locally built cabs. P. M. Cassart's lorry is, incidentally, captioned both Mk 6 and Mk 5L and is known to have been chassis number 2/L 31951 with P6 engine number 3,230,249.

The Seddon PSV range was becoming increasingly important and as well as the 32 seat Mk 4 included the very similar but longer 35 seat Mk 6 (the 1952 example here is registered RPJ 312). The traditional radiator was often deleted by coach-builders seeking up-to-the-minute styling. Then in 1953 came a smaller P4 engined 7P model for 28 seats on "light riding routes" exemplified here by the exported bus registered BB 7925. Then followed the Mk 10 13′ 11″ wheelbase and Mk 11 16′ 6″ wheelbase under-floor engined bus soon known as the Pennine. Its frontal styling had first appeared on a Mk 7 three-tonner at the end of 1950. For the first time it used vertical mid-mounted Perkins P6 79 bhp or R6 108 bhp engines. A Mk 10 is shown with 9 Special on its destination blind as well as a chassis view.

# Seddon Diesel
## Mark 12 . . . . . normal control

*Photographs on this and the previous page:*

Seddon went both up and down the weight scale in 1954. The little Twenty Five (its payload in hundredweight) had a Perkins P3 diesel and is shown here as a fourteen-seat personnel carrier. The Mk 12 had an all-metal cab and was for eight-ton loads primarily in export territories. It could have Leyland 0375 and Perkins R6 or P6 followed by Leyland 0400 and Perkins 6:354. GVW with the larger Leyland engine went up to 14 tons.

Leyland also supplied engines to Dodge and Bedford at the time as well. of course, to Albion which it had owned since 1948, and Scammell which it acquired in 1955. An interesting anecdote about the Twenty Five concerns its first appearance in *Commercial Motor* when Brian Hatton of *Commercial Motors* did a cutaway drawing from Seddon's drawings before a vehicle was completed. Seddon was so appalled by how they saw it was going to look that they re-designed it there and then!

Amongst many early dealers who both benefited themselves and Seddon by becoming involved with the new marque was Halls of Finchley. Here we have a couple of views of Halls' premises in the 1950s. Amongst their best customers were Metal Box, C&A Modes, Belling, W. H. Cullen, William Moss & Sons, Cyprien Fox and J. Hollins & Sons (who had their cabs built locally) and there were of course numerous one-off sales including an R6 underfloor engined coach to Ted Heath and his Band. All the vehicles in the pictures are by Seddon except for a lone Perkins engined Vulcan in the workshop and the Standard Vanguard service van outside.

*Photographs on this page and overleaf:*
In 1954 Atkinson published a brochure specifically covering its export range. Many of these vehicles were shipped as bare chassis for fitment with bodies and cabs overseas, a particularly flamboyant six-wheeler being shown here by courtesy of Niels Jansen. The ones shipped complete from Britain usually had all-steel cabs, which were sometimes divisible at the waist-line to reduce height.

Double-Deck Passenger
Vehicle Chassis
Model PD.746

The Knight of the Road

The Atkinson double deck PD.746 chassis is shown here in a March 1956 catalogue. They had vertical front mounted 6LW engines and five-speed constant mesh gearboxes. The local SHMD Board bought one of them but the other proved difficult to sell and Atkinson made no further attempts at this particular market.

This 1948 Atkinson had a spectacular accident in 1959 when the driver left it parked in Sheffield to telephone for his delivery instructions. When he returned it had run away and leapt into a garden, luckily causing only minimal damage!

In the early 1950s roughly ninety percent of the 25 chassis being made by Atkinson per month were six- and eight-wheelers. The 6LX 150 bhp engine ultimately replaced the 6LW in the largest models and Atkinson was the first company to standardise air brakes on all axles. It also led the trend to fabrications rather than castings to save weight and simplify changes to specification.

*Photographs on the previous page:*

If home-market Atkinsons looked rather archaic in the mid 1950s, then many of their rivals from Seddon most certainly did not. Since 1954 Seddon had been a pioneer user of fibreglass in its cab construction and this permitted various complex shapes. Shown here is a 1957 14 tons gross Mk 14 tipper, a type usually fitted with Gardner 5LW engine. The even more futuristic Mark 15 for 11 tons GVW belonging to Glasgow & District Motorways was a model introduced at the 1956 Commercial Motor Show and usually was powered by the R6 diesel, though the 4LW and Leyland 0375 were added. Also at the Show was the new three-axle Mark 12 F/6 for 16 tons GVW with 5 or 6LW diesels.

*Photographs below and overleaf:*

If some Seddons looked futuristic, then the traditional model continued to be built much as it had always appeared.

Spillers had dozens in its fleet, the one here dating from 1956. The STC dropsider was new a year earlier.

A few Seddons were fitted with wrapround screen Holmalloy cabs and Woodstock Factory soon introduced a similar looking cab in fibreglass but retaining the aluminium radiator. Shown is a 1954 tractive unit used by the Post Office and now preserved.

MKA 812 dates from 1951 and is shown when still in service 25 years later.

Photographs on this page and overleaf:

An assortment of classic Atkinsons, including J. Barrett's 1957 Chinese six that regularly returned 15 mpg thanks to its 5LW. The other twin steer six-wheeler dates from 1959 whilst the eight-wheel tankers are 1956 with standard cab and 1955 with all-metal cab in Kennings' service. The 1953 registered wrecker with later cab is shown at work in 1978 whilst the tractive unit is unusual in being specifically for use with Scammell self-coupling semi trailers. It could have 4 or 5 LW engines developing 75 to 94 bhp.

Some more unusual looking Atkinsons, this time from a 1957 advertisement. That year marked Atkinson's all-out attempt to offer "Rangeability" to emulate Scammell in the special vehicle market. Accordingly the drawing office staff was increased and all manner of unlikely projects were undertaken. These included half-cab dumptrucks to rival Foden and enormous Omega tractors for the oil industry. Then there were crane carriers and all-wheel driven chassis for many purposes.

The dumptrucks had as standard 6LX engines in the 9/10 cu. yd. (though a larger body is shown here) 1366 series and 5 or 6 LW in the 6/7 cu. yd. 745/6. However, the new British built Cummins engines were offered in both and regularly specified on account of the 164 bhp they offered. Even more power was available with 210 bhp Rolls-Royce or Cummins units. The six-wheeler had a six-speed gearbox and the four-wheeler five-speeds. The cab was of all-steel construction and bodywork came from various outside suppliers such as Telehoist, Autolifts and Edbro.

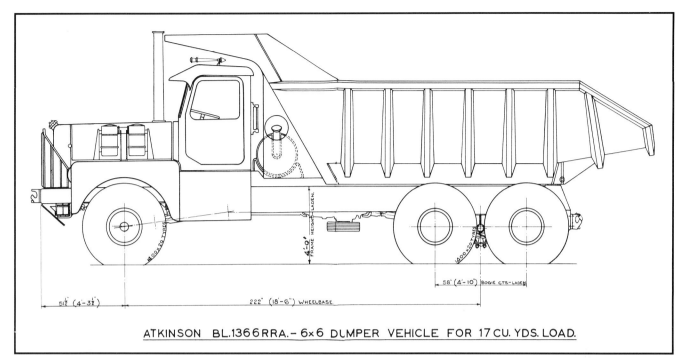

ATKINSON BL.1366RRA. – 6×6 DUMPER VEHICLE FOR 17 CU. YDS. LOAD.

The Omega was conceived as the result of an enquiry from Aramco in the Middle East and started life with Rolls-Royce C6.SFL supercharged diesels and Self Changing Gears eight-speed transmissions. The first three ran at 90 tons GTW in Saudi Arabia. Then came versions with Rolls-Royce engines and five-speed automatic gearboxes. Currency difficulties restricted sales and the last of these impressive machines was delivered in 1960. On test the 64,000 lbs. drawbar pull was found to pull out rear crossmembers like matchsticks! The chassis diagram of an Omega dumper is interesting as it was sent to the author in September 1959 but never existed in the flesh.

Seddon too was looking towards the heavy end of the market and was also willing to build "specials". A salesman of Greek origin wanted some six-wheelers with ultra high capacity front axles and the bonnetted 6 x 4 Sirdar M of 1958 was the result. It had a British built Cummins 168 bhp diesel and Fuller Roadranger ten-speed gearbox.

Seddon was amongst the first to specify Cummins diesels though other models at the 1958 Commercial Motor Show featured Gardner, Leyland and Perkins engines as well as a horizontal AEC AH410 in a new Pennine single deck chassis.

Another and more profitable use for the new Cummins engine turned out to be in the DD8 rigid eight-wheeler introduced by Seddon in 1958. Some had Gardners and all had power-assisted steering and five-speed constant-mesh gearboxes with double-drive worm axles and third differentials. Also available was the SD or single drive version as well as 6 x 2 and 6 x 4 types, often with Leyland engines. Rear suspension was usually by two pairs of semi-elliptics joined together in line by balance beams. However, a Maxartic twin spring system was later offered for increased wheel movement on off-road work. A 1959 Cummins engined DD8 is shown.

*Photographs on the following four pages and top of page 51:*
Now that Seddon had entered the heavy market they were in headlong conflict with Atkinson and its rivals. Atkinson chose 1958, the same year that the DD8 came on the scene, to introduce its now familiar fibreglass cab with wrap-round windscreens. Most were for maximum legal weight operation and usually had Gardner engines, though some Cummins and Rolls-Royce types were utilised. A 14 ton gross rigid four-wheeler joined the range in 1959 and in 1963 the Weightmaster range looked much as before but unladen weight had been reduced without sacrificing strength and 112 bhp Perkins engines were available in the lightest models.

Shown are an assortment of early types including a 1960 M&B tanker, 1959 truck mixer, 1960 articulated machinery carrier, 1959 four axle tipper, a pair of 1958 flat bed eight-wheelers with bolsters for girder transport and a 6 x 4 low loader with knock-out axle semi-trailer. The layout diagram is of a TS 1065/6 series twin-steer model available with 5 or 6LW engine. Its specification included five-speed constant mesh gearbox (6- and 10-speed also available), aluminium radiator with detachable Withnell tubes, 16" dry plate clutch, overhead worm axle, air brakes, Marles cam and roller steering and 24 volt electrical system.

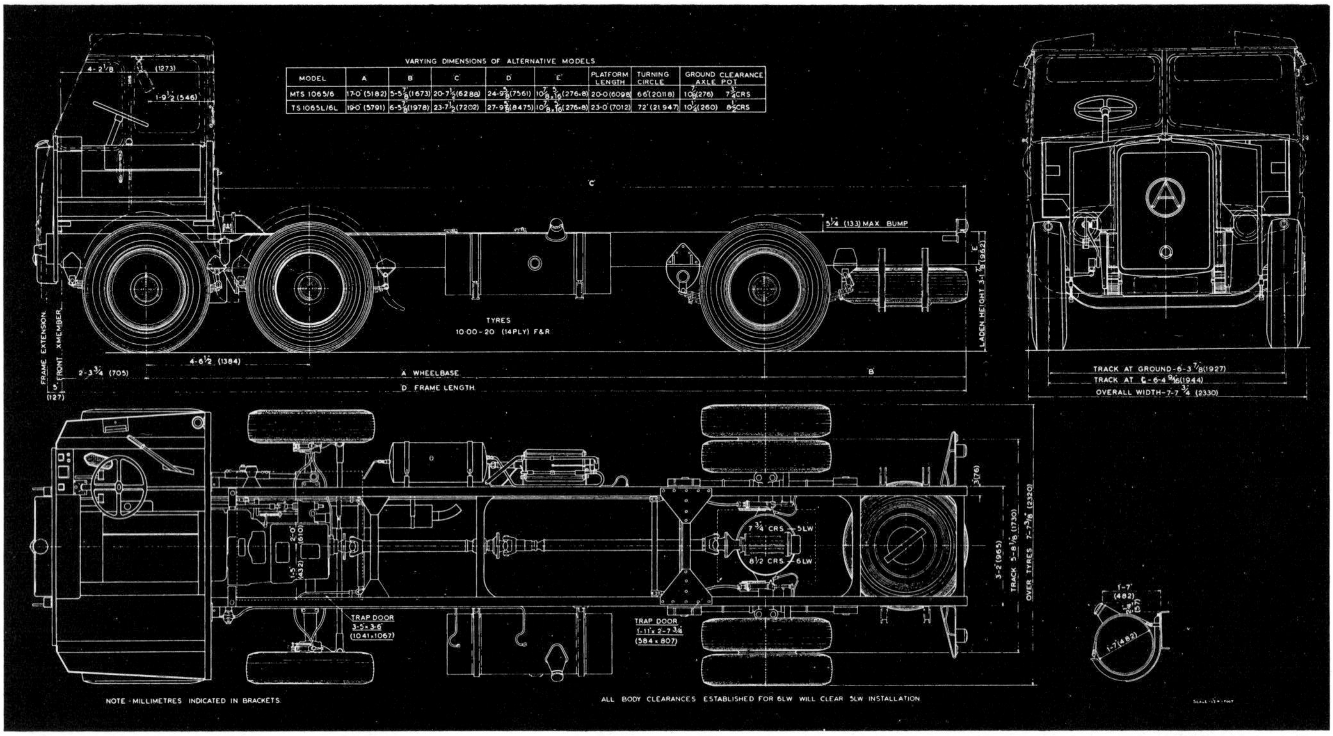
VARYING DIMENSIONS OF ALTERNATIVE MODELS
MODEL | A | B | C | D | E | PLATFORM LENGTH | TURNING CIRCLE | GROUND CLEARANCE AXLE POT
MTS 1065/6 | 17-0 (5182) | 5-5 7/8 (1673) | 20-7 1/2 (6288) | 24-9 5/8 (7561) | 10 7/8 x 5/16 (276x8) | 20-0 (6098) | 66' (20.118) | 10 7/8 (276) 7 3/4 CRS
TS 1065L/6L | 19-0 (5791) | 6-5 7/8 (1978) | 23-7 1/2 (7202) | 27-9 5/8 (8475) | 10 7/8 x 5/16 (276x8) | 23-0 (7012) | 72' (21.947) | 10 1/4 (260) 8 1/2 CRS
4-2 1/8 (1273)
1-9 1/2 (546)
5 1/4 (133) MAX BUMP
TYRES
10.00-20 (14PLY) F&R
FRAME EXTENSION
FRONT XMEMBER
2-3 3/4 (705)
4-6 1/2 (1384)
A WHEELBASE
D FRAME LENGTH
LADEN HEIGHT
TRACK AT GROUND-6-3 7/8 (1927)
OVERALL WIDTH-7-7 3/4 (2330)
TRAP DOOR 3-5 x 3-6 (1041 x 1067)
TRAP DOOR 1-11 x 2-7 3/4 (584 x 807)
5LW
6LW
OVER TYRES 7-7 3/8 (2320)
NOTE - MILLIMETRES INDICATED IN BRACKETS.
ALL BODY CLEARANCES ESTABLISHED FOR 6LW WILL CLEAR 5LW INSTALLATION

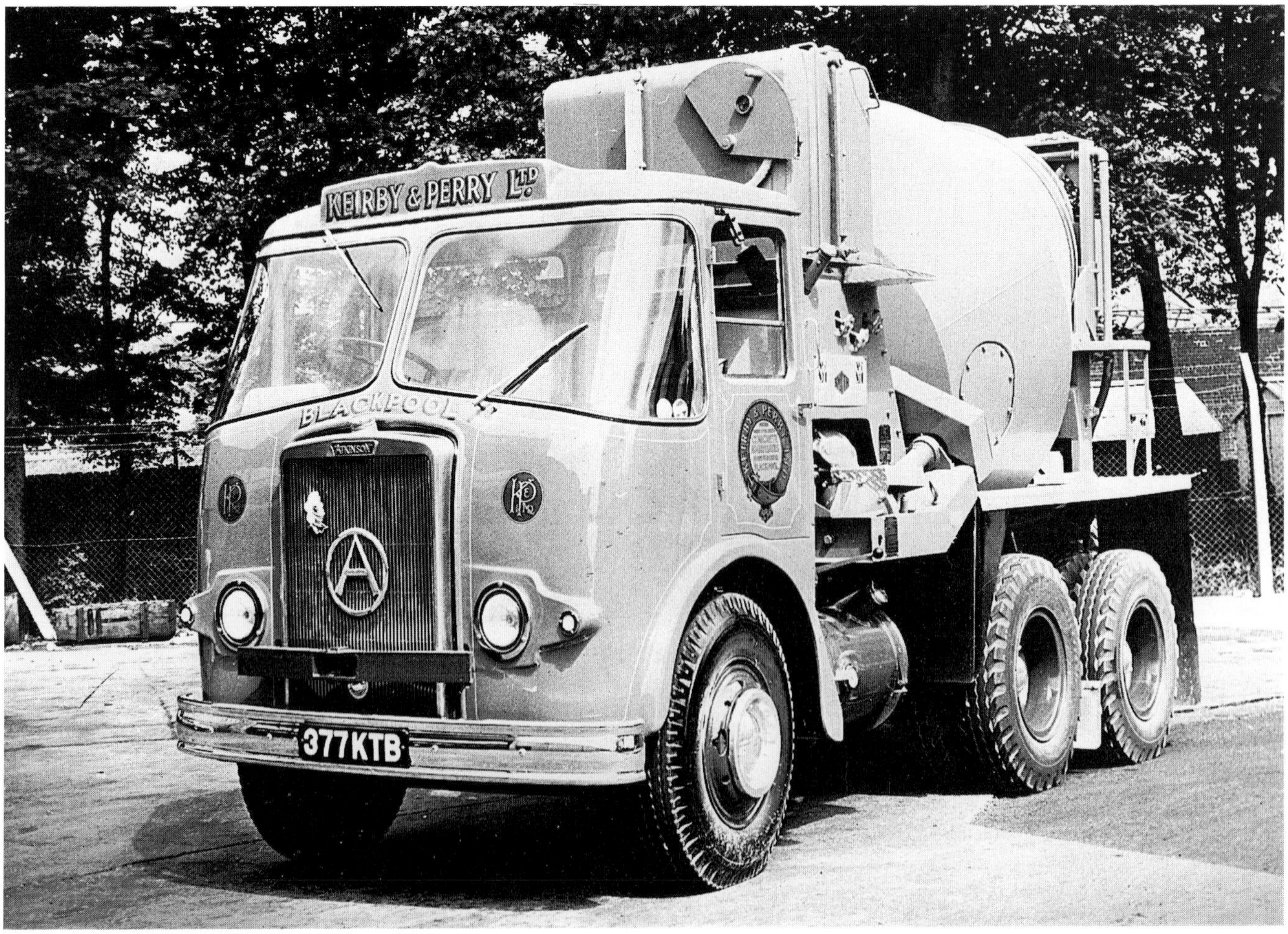
KEIRBY & PERRY LTD
BLACKPOOL
ATKINSON
377 KTB

Seddon's expansion into so many weight ranges at the end of the 1950s caused all manner of problems to the over-stretched company. Amongst these were spares supply and the training of suitable service mechanics. In the end a rationalised range evolved in 1962 but before that it was possible to buy all shapes and sizes of Seddon with various different fibreglass cabs. By way of example we see here a 1960 heavy duty artic about to carry Bluebird to the United States for its Land Speed Record bid. This truck had one of the first Shotts-built Cummins engines to be fitted to a road vehicle and the cab style also used on the biggest six- and eight-wheelers. Then there is a 1962 advertisement for the 16 ton gvw tractor and a lighter 10/12 ton 1961 artic with Boden semi-trailer made in a factory close to that of Seddon. Also shown are a 7 ton integral van supplied by Halls of Finchley in 1959 and a 1962 street sweeper with Lewin equipment. The Seven Tonner usually had Leyland 0.350 power until the launch of the new Perkins direct injection 6.354 in 1960.

# 16 ton G.V.W.

## Tractor Permits 28' 6"

## Trailer Length

Follow the example of the fleet operators and invest in the Seddon traditions of sturdy, lasting workmanship. The 16 G.V.W. Tractor has an extremely robust chassis, which, together with its economy of running, makes it the ideal prime mover—for local and inter-city running! Its newly-styled cab offers superior driving comfort and well positioned controls.

The short chassis length of this tractor permits 28' 6" trailer length—inside the legal maximum—and a turning circle of under 30 ft. Choice of 350 engine with 5 or 6 speed gear box and 354 engine with 5 speed gear box; two speed or spiral bevel rear axle. This outstanding tractor design will take any type of automatic or 5th wheel gear, and all standard trailer lengths up to 28' 6". Long front springs give excellent riding both laden and unladen.

### NEW HIGH IN TRAILER CAPACITY

Model illustrated is a "Carrimore" 28' 6" trailer fitted with rising roof, operated by a simple cam mechanism. This vehicle makes an ideal pallet transporter —the 28' 6" trailer taking banks of seven 4 ft. pallets and the rising roof ensuring the load is always a snug fit.

## SEDDON DIESEL VEHICLES LTD., WOODSTOCK FACTORY OLDHAM.
### Telephone: Manchester Main 6041 (8 lines)

*Details from the manufacturers, Seddon Diesel Vehicles Limited. Tel:- Manchester MAIn 6041 (8 lines) or from your local Distributor.*
*London Sales:- Halls of Finchley Ltd., Tel:- Hillside 1044/9*
*London Service and Spares:- Arcadia Avenue, Finchley Central, N.3. Tel:- Finchley 5908/9 and 0096*

*Photographs on this and opposite page top:* Atkinson's specials continued to take up a disproportionate amount of time and space at the factory. Apart from the dumptrucks the only ones to be made in substantial numbers (over 400) were the MoT 6 x 6 snowplough/gritters for the new Motorways. These carried Altkinson's of Clitheroe equipment (not connected with

Atkinson Vehicles Ltd.) and used Cummins NHE 180 diesels and the first load compensated braking system to be found as standard on a British vehicle. Here we see an example on test in the Alps accompanied by Berliet and MAN snowploughs.

The original prototype used Cummins V8 engines with Allison automatic transmissions, but the in-line six-cylinder 12.17 litre Cummins and ZF six-speed manual combination were chosen for production. Some chassis were also built with 8 x 6 drive and the example shown has an AEC engine.

*Photograph below:* Although the big Omega tractors had not been a commercial success Atkinson, for some long forgotten reason, acquired the remains of the equally unfortunate Rotinoff heavy tractor concern in about 1962. Since 1960 this had been known as Lomount Vehicles and Engineering and had made Atlantic and Super Atlantic Rolls-Royce powered machines. Shown is an Atkinson brochure of 1963 for them with an artist-applied "A" on the radiator. Very few of these 366 or 275 bhp vehicles, which could have 6 x 4 or 6 x 6, were sold under the aegis of Atkinson.

The Knight of the Road.

**ATKINSON VEHICLES LTD**
WINERY LANE
WALTON-LE-DALE
PRESTON

TELEPHONE 84284-5-6-7
TELEX 67543

London Sales and Service:
NIGHTINGALE ENGINEERING CO. LTD.,
Western Lane, Nightingale Lane, S.W.12.
TELEPHONE: KELVIN 2193-4-5-6. TELEX 21121.

ATKINSON VEHICLES (Scotland) LTD.,
Carlisle Road Airdrie.
TELEPHONE: OFFICE & NIGHT: AIRDRIE 2881.

The following seven photographs:
Whilst Atkinson's Rangeability was leading to more and more models, Seddon decided to take the opposite route at the end of 1962 with its rationalised range. The old Mark numbers disappeared and were replaced by a lettering system with three groups of digits. The first gave the gross weight, the second the number of wheels (with DD added if double-drive) and the third the type of engine – for example 16-4-354 meaning 16 tons, 4 wheels and (6)354 Perkins. Many parts were interchangeable, including Seddon's own hub reduction nine-ton drive axle. Assembly was speeded and as a result Seddon was soon building over a thousand vehicles per year. Shown are an assortment of the new simplified models, some of which continued to use the two-spring Maxartic bogie. The four- and six-wheel rigids had Perkins, Leyland or Gardner engines, the heavy four-wheel tractive units Gardner or AEC engines, and the lighter ones Perkins, Leyland or Gardner engines.

*The following four photographs:*

After building 170 passenger chassis over fourteen years, Atkinson abandoned them in the mid 1960s. Some of the last are shown here in the shape of some Perkins engined 26 seaters in Cyprus and an unusual 4 x 4 chassis with 6LX engine, David Brown five-speed gearbox, and ZF transfer box for use on non-existent roads in Mozambique. There were also some conventional six-wheel truck chassis with soft springs for use with bus bodywork in Portuguese East Africa and a final batch of underfloor Gardner engined semi-automatic gearbox single-deckers for Sunderland. The piece of letterhead from 1963 shows that passenger chassis were still theoretically in the programe and also lists the directors. B. F. Caunt was to die in 1967, when his position was taken by P. M. Yates.

The brochure is dated May 1963 but amusingly enough shows one of the earliest underfloor engined buses dating from 1951.

TELEPHONE Nº 84284-5-6-7 TELEX NO. 67543
NIGHT SERVICE - 84284

REGISTERED TRADE MARK

TELEGRAMS:"WAGONS, PRESTON."
SPARES - AFTER 6 P.M. PHONE 56217

# ATKINSON VEHICLES LIMITED

DIRECTORS W G ALLEN, F C A (CHAIRMAN) B FRANCIS CAUNT, A M I MECH E M S A E (MANAGING DIRECTOR)
W C PARK A A C C A (SECRETARY) P BURGESS A.W. ALLEN, F C A P M YATES F R COWELL

## MANUFACTURERS OF "ATKINSON" FREIGHT AND PASSENGER VEHICLES

WINERY LANE
WALTON-LE-DALE

NR. PRESTON

LONDON OFFICE & SERVICE STATION: WESTERN LANE, NIGHTINGALE LANE, S.W.12. TELEPHONE: BATTERSEA 2193

## PASSENGER CHASSIS

### Model P.L. 745 H

ATKINSON VEHICLES LTD., WALTON-LE-DALE, PRESTON, ENGLAND.

Despite the rationalised Seddon range there was still room for some variations, as shown by this 12,000 litre tanker supplied by Belgian distributor Hocké (which also handled Steyr commercials). It is a 14-4-400 model with 140 bhp Leyland engine. De Boever's already had twelve similar tankers in use when this one entered service in 1963.

The Knight of the Road

## FOUR WHEELED
## SEMI-BONNETED
## TRACTOR CHASSIS

Model SBT. 946. XA.

**ATKINSON VEHICLES LTD., WINERY LANE, WALTON-LE-DALE, Nr. PRESTON, ENGLAND.**

Some heavy road tractors more closely based on the standard range but with normal control were built at Walton le Dale in the 1960s. A series of 25 ton capacity Scammell-type model was built for Pickfords in 1962 with Gardner 6LX 150 bhp engines and six-speed gearboxes with double-reduction axles. These were followed by a 40/50 ton 6 x 4 version primarily for export. These had Rolls-Royce 210 bhp or Cummins 212 bhp engines as standard or else up to 335 bhp engines by either firm with automatic or manual transmission. A 6 x 6 type was also offered. The 100 ton GTW truck shown was at the 1968 Commercial Motor Show and had a Cummins NH 250 engine and Allison transmission.

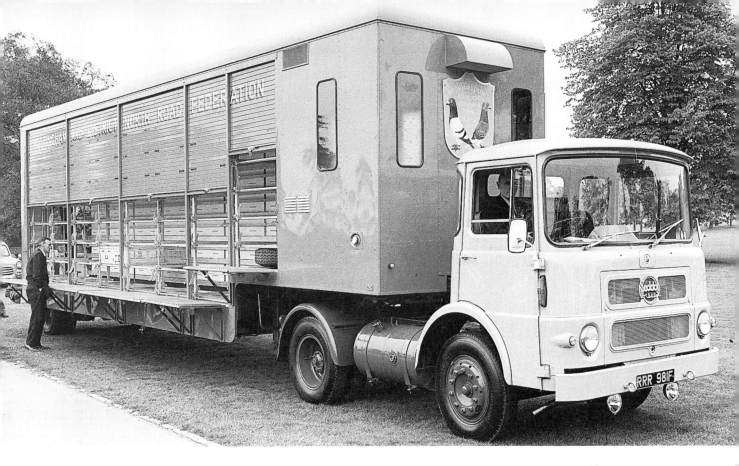

Photographs on this page and overleaf:

Next in Seddon's rationalisation programme came the 13:Four in late 1964 which was a remarkably cheap (initially £1,710 as chassis/cab) "assembled" vehicle utilising a steel "Supa-Cab" from Motor Panels in Coventry that was also to be seen with different grilles on several other makes of truck. The engine used was the Perkins 6.354 mated to a specially designed David Brown five-speed gearbox. Quarter inch steel sheet was used for the pressed chassis, the drive axle was by Seddon and air brakes were standard. Payload was over nine tons dependant on weight of bodywork. Some early examples of the extremely successful 13:Four or 20:Four as it was called as an artic, are shown. The six-wheeler was a Primrose conversion for 17 tons GCW. Note also the left-hand drive 13:Four for export.

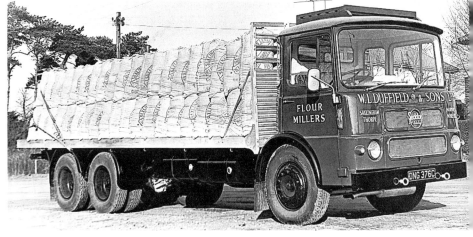

*Photographs this page and overleaf:*

In 1963 Atkinson briefly tried to woo operators away from the traditional radiator typified by the Suttons/AETS artic, with the grille shown on the two bow fronted vehicles. Sales were disappointing so the radiator was allowed to live on! Interestingly enough, Atkinson also continued to offer metal panelled coachbuilt cabs long after the wrap-round screen fibreglass type arrived. This Pickfords tanker dates from 1961. All the vehicles shown had Gardner 150 bhp engines except the low-loader, which tried one of Ruston's air-cooled types. Atkinson had rationalised its road haulage range somewhat and from late 1965 now called tractors Silver Knights, freighters and tankers Black Knights and tippers/mixers Gold Knights.

The specialised Atkinson range now contained some crane carrier chassis. The half cab types date from 1961 and could have Perkins, Gardner or Cummins engines with David Brown or ZF gearboxes. They had solid equaliser beams at the rear in place of springs. The low cab type was a new model in 1966 and was powered by a Perkins V8 for the first time, which was situated above and behind the front axle. The cab enabled two or three people to be carried with the jib over the cab roof.

*Photographs on these pages and overleaf:*
Some heavier Seddon models received the Motor Panels cab in 1965 with the arrival of the
16:Four and derivatives. These had Perkins V8 170 bhp diesels and could also be had as
22 ton six-wheelers with Unipower or Primrose third axles. Articulated versions went up to
28 tons GTW in 1967 with the V8 engine. Twin line brakes were standardised. The 16:Four
badge in place of the usual Seddon Diesel badge only appeared on early examples. The
truckmixer shown had Thompson/Stetter 5 cu. yd. drum and grossed 15 tons 8 cwt.

*The following seven photographs:*
Atkinson continued to have thriving export sales and an assortment from the 1960s are shown here. The 6 x 6 chassis was destined for life as a 22 ton airfield crash tender in Australia. The BP tanker also worked in Australia and had a 6LW engine, six-speed gearbox, double-reduction axle and steel cab. The 135 foot long load is in Australia in 1962 being hauled by a 210 bhp Rolls-Royce engined tractor. The six-wheeler towing a two axle Fruehauf tanker trailer is a Detroit V8 318 bhp engined outfit in South Africa with Allison transmission, Kirkstall axles, ZF power steering and Clayton Dewandre twin line brakes. The Silver Knight carrying two D8 tractors in Jamaica had a Cummins 220 diesel and ZF six-speed box. The logging lorries are in New Zealand and have 6LXB engines. The six-wheel Silver Knight with six tons of concrete ballast is towing a 290 ton load in Jamaica. It had Cummins C250 diesel, Kirkstall bogie and Allison gearbox.

DANGER
135' LONG 16' WIDE LOAD
UNDER ESCORT

*The following nine photographs:*

Late in 1967 Atkinson redesigned the classic cab to create a Mk 2 version. This was six inches wider, had a two inch lower doorline, a completely flat floor, improved interior, lock actuators in place of handbrake to ease access, and dual headlamps. The pedal position was improved, a Chapman suspension seat standardised, and heater output increased. The factory was booming under chief engineer J. E. Cooke and sales director S. Eden-Smith (shown) with sales of 1,033 chassis in twelve months of 1967/8 compared with 979 in the previous year. P. M. Yates took over as managing director in 1967, the year in which the sixteen-thousandth Atki was made, and he instituted the move of the service department and spares store to Bamber Bridge to make more room for assembly at Vinery Lane. Most of the Mk 2 vehicles shown will be familiar, except perhaps the twin steer tractive unit, a new model in 1967, and the Esso four-wheel tanker, which was one of a small number of special low tare weight trucks powered by Detroit diesels.

**S. EDEN-SMITH   SALES DIRECTOR**

**J. E. COOKE   CHIEF ENGINEER**

74

*Photographs on this and following two pages:*

Another attempt at designing an acceptable alternative to the Mk 1 came at the 1964 Commercial Motor Show. It was called the Guardsman and appeared in the livery of Bulwark. It was of timber and metal construction with plastics panelling and was fitted with a Cummins 235 bhp V8 diesel. Not many vehicles were sold with the Guardsman cab and the next attempt to lose the traditional radiator came with the high and shallow Viewline cab. This appeared at the 1966 Commercial Motor Show with rather untidy grille, but in production normally had a shell resembling a traditional radiator. Once again, few vehicles were sold with this striking looking cab.

*Photographs on these pages and overleaf:*

Early in 1966 Seddon realised that it was going to need a bigger tractor for the new 32 ton regulations and the resulting 32:Four was launched late in 1967 with Rolls-Royce Eagle 220 engine and David Brown six-speed gearbox. It was designed with 38 ton operation in mind and chassis/cab price was a mere £3,875. It is shown here as it was originally envisaged with Seddon spelt out across the top of the grille, and how it actually appeared in service. The other views are of an engine being installed at Woodstock Factory and a general glimpse of the cramped assembly area.

The annual accounts to 30th June, 1968, showed pre-tax profits of £520,000 and D. W., H. and G. J. Redmond, H. Seddon, P. J. Verdellis and E. Sayer as directors. This was the last year in which Herbert Seddon was a director and was also the year in which Robert Hesketh Seddon, the original designer, died. Production in the following years was up 19.4 percent at 2,500 vehicles, making Seddon the largest independent British commercial vehicle manufacturer. Its employees numbered over a thousand compared with five hundred before the launch of the 13:Four.

**3**

A newcomer in late 1968 was a 2,000 cu. ft. van version of the Seddon passenger chassis (the Pennine IV PSV normally had a 6.354 litre engine though the V8 Perkins was optional), with bodywork by Pennine Coachcraft, the Seddon subsidiary. Other subsidiaries were the distributors Halls (Finchley) Ltd., Seddon Diesel of Rhodesia which was lying dormant due to sanctions, and the newly formed Seddon-Deutz Ltd., a £50,000 company in which Seddon held half the shares.

The Seddon-Deutz Ltd. formed in 1968 stemmed from an exchange of engineering and export information agreed between Seddon and its chief engineer Walter Booth (who became a director in 1969), and Klöckner-Humboldt-Deutz in September 1966. A separate factory was established at Middleton, Manchester, to fit Seddons with Deutz engines primarily for export and to assemble the familiar bonneted Magirus-Deutz 6 x 4 and 6 x 6 site vehicles (a 14 cu. yd. Telehoist equipped dumper is shown).

The venture was not a commercial success and was sold to the Magirus-Deutz importer in the early 1970s, after which the firm moved to Winsford, Cheshire. The Seddon-types shown are an early chassis/cab and a 120 bhp six-cylinder tilt van with ZF five-speed synchromesh gearbox used in 1971 for collecting components from Ulm. The latter carried British tyres on the outward journey for fitment to Magirus-Deutz trucks.

Meanwhile Atkinson also tried a German association of a different sort when it bought steel tilt cabs from Krupp, which had discontinued its road haulage range. In July 1968 Atkinson Vehicles (Europe) was established between Antwerp and Brussels with A. W. Allen, P. M. Yates, S. Eden-Smith (who had been apprenticed at Leyland and had worked for Sentinel from 1953 to 1956) and R. Van Pelt as directors. 26 and 38 tonne models were offered from 1969 with Eagle 220 and 260 diesels, ZF gearboxes and Kirkstall axles. Sadly this brave attempt at breaking into the European market was not a commercial success, though the Silver Knight vehicles themselves performed well. An illustration from a 1969 press release is shown together with a photograph of a Krupp with the same cab in its tilted position to gain access to its Cummins 185 bhp V6.

Atkinson had set up various overseas subsidiaries and in the 1960s increased its Lancashire facilities with the acquisition of Atherton Bros., general engineers who also made concrete mixers for truck chassis. Their construction methods suited the assembly of dumptrucks and these vehicles had become known as Hylodes in 1965 when Peter Hamilton Equipment Ltd. placed a one-million pound order and became distributor for Hylodes. Peter Hamilton is shown at the wheel of the chassis with Peter M. Yates, Atkinson's managing director on terra firma. 10 and 14 cu. yd. versions were offered, usually with Cummins engines. Full and half cab versions are shown alongside each other at Crystal Palace in 1965. Some heavy slag carriers and dumptrucks were also built on four axle chassis as well as ultra heavy duty tractors. One of the latter is shown handling a rival Euclid dumptruck.

Various chassis, notably Fords, were converted to all-wheel-drive by AWD of Camberley, then Bilston and finally Swindon. Various Supa-Cab Seddons received the AWD treatment and here are two of the results. The six-wheeler with reinforced frame was fitted with container handling equipment.

Seddon and Atkinson were now in headlong conflict with an increasing proportion of the former's business at the heavy end of the market. Both firms used a high proportion of bought-in components and though Atkinson had more of a quality image there was in fact not a lot to choose between them in engineering quality, especially as Seddon's vehicles were substantially cheaper and had steel cabs. Here we have a couple of maximum weight 32:Four Seddons, BFL 840K being particularly interesting as it was the testbed for the application of a Perkins V8 and was running in the Perkins Engines fleet.

Atkinson's assembly operations in Australia commenced in 1962 and a half share in the enterprise was held for a time by the haulage firm of Mayne Nickless (one of whose heavy haulage units is shown). In 1966 an Australian built fibreglass tilt cab (by Reinforced Plastics Pty. Ltd.) was adopted and an example (the rigid eight chassis shown) was brought to Britain in 1968 for evaluation. From 1965 until his death in 1971 J. M. MacInnes ran the Australian (and later New Zealand) companies, having started working for Atkinson at Airdrie in Scotland in 1959. The other Australian Atkinsons shown here include a milk tanker with rubber suspension, a 7,000 gallon Caltex tanker with 290 bhp Detroit 8V71 diesel, Fuller fifteen-speed Roadranger gearbox, and Rockwell bogie, and a rigid eight with trailer working in New Guinea. It had a Cummins 250 bhp diesel with turbocharger to maintain power at 12,000 feet, a thirteen-speed Roadranger and Kirkstall bogie. Finally there is one of seven Shell roadtrains which started work in 1969 carrying 19,500 gallons of fuel. They were powered by 335 bhp Cummins diesels with thirteen-speed Roadrangers and Kirkstall Omega bogies. They worked the thousand mile Stuart Highway from Darwin to Alice Springs, spending much of the time taking detours through the bush to avoid washed-out sections.

In 1969 Atkinson replaced the traditional cast aluminium radiator surround with a fibreglass replica and here we see an advertisement that appeared that November which attempted to counter criticism of the non-steel cab by claiming it to be safer. Also shown is a Fertiliquids artic of the same year and an eight-wheeler out to pasture in Robert Fossett's circus yard in Northamptonshire in 1986. The Atkinson Vehicles Ltd. business was looking very attractive to rivals and in 1970 ERF and Foden fought for its control. Leyland already held about twenty percent of Atkinson's shares and in November 1970 it came down in favour of a bid from Seddon which valued Atkinson at £4.8 million. Though the lighter models from Seddon added to Atkinson's heavyweight expertise made commercial sense, it caused ructions at Walton le Dale where the staff were fiercely proud and independent. Chief engineer J. E. Cooke headed to ERF and sales director S. Eden Smith, A. Allen (whose family had originally acquired Atkinson) and P. M. Yates all left the firm, along with several other staff members, in the course of the next year.

# John M—— is a good driver. He's just been fired. He refused to drive the other vehicles.

He just had to go. There were other trucks in the fleet and he'd driven them all, but John was becoming more and more adamant about driving only the Atkinsons. Then came the accident. He wasn't hurt, but he could have been. The truck in front of him broke a spring and shed part of its load. The road was slippery and there was a lot of traffic. John wan't able to avoid everything but the Atkinson "coped better than anything else that I've ever driven could have done." He stopped straight, but a vehicle coming the other way slewed round and slammed into his cab. "Steel would have closed in on me—I've always worried about that," he said, but the glass fibre, ash-framed cab on the Atkinson just fractured and split. After this incident John stuck to his guns and wouldn't drive anything but Atkinsons. "They've got the power too, and they're reliable," he says. Well, now he's getting what he wants—a job in an all Atkinson fleet. They're getting what *they* want too—another good driver. Atkinsons tend to attract the good drivers in any fleet.

# ATKINSON BUILD·IN MORE

ATKINSON VEHICLES LTD., WALTON-LE-DALE, PRESTON, LANCS. PR5 4AS. TEL: PRESTON 58211   N. V. ATKINSON VEHICLES (EUROPE) S.A., 42 BOOMSESTEENWEG, AARTSELAAR, BELGIUM.
ATKINSON VEHICLES (LONDON) LTD., BALHAM, LONDON, S.W.12. TEL: 01-673 2193   ATKINSON VEHICLES (SCOTLAND) LTD., CARLISLE ROAD, AIRDRIE, SCOTLAND. TEL: AIRDRIE 2881

*Photographs on these pages and overleaf:*

At the 1970 Commercial Motor Show, whilst the battle for its ownership raged and Tom Kirby became director of manufacturing, Atkinson gave all its models names to replace the old type names that had lapsed. Two-axle tractors were called Borderer, twin-steer tractors Leader, 6 x 4 tractors Venturer (they were originally reported in the Press as "Adventurers"), 6 x 4 rigids Searcher, and eight-wheelers Defender.

Shown is a September 1970 Leader chassis for 38 tons GTW with the new Gardner 8LXB engine. It had a nine-speed Roadranger box and Kirkstall hub reduction axle. The 1971 6 x 4 50 tons GTW outfit with King trailer for Pickfords also had a 240 bhp Gardner and was by now called the Venturer. Goodier's prototype eight-wheeler was one of a revised range plated at 26, 28 or 30 tons in late 1971. They had Gardner 6LXB engines, David Brown six-speed constant-mesh gearboxes and Seddon hub reduction axles on the single drives or Eaton on the doubles. The model names seem to have confused Atkinson as much as operators judging by the 180 bhp Gardner engined brick lorry which should be a Searcher, as it is not a tractive unit, but is badged Defender! The Borderer is shown with a 4,500 gallon Thompson Trailmobile wine tanker.

*The following nine photographs:*

With Seddon's bid accepted, Harry Redmond (shown overleaf) became chairman and managing director (a position soon held by G.J. Redmond) and in August 1971 a new logo of interwined circles was adopted. To July that year the twelve months tax paid profits had risen to £650,000 (including six months' contribution from Atkinson) and sales director P.J. Verdelliss reported that short-time working, that was affecting the whole industry, ended in November. Even so the following year's after-tax profits were down to £80,000. There was little apparent rationalisation between the two ranges to begin with apart from the Seddon axle under some Atkinsons, and the Supa-Cab on some export Atkinsons, like the 230 bhp Cummins engined Venturer with King low bed trailer for Sri Lanka. The rear view shows the steel and plastic cabbed Atkinsons compared in March 1972. In November 1971 the Perkins V8 powered tractor (shown earlier in prototype form) was launched at £4,850, making it the cheapest 32-tonner available. At the same time a 24:Four six-cylinder Perkins turbo was offered at £3,625. Also in 1972 a twin-steer 34:Six was developed with Primrose for export markets (an example for Poland with Crane Fruehauf cement tank is shown) along with 16:Four 6LXB powered drawbar outfits, and a 38:Four with sleeper cab launched at Brussels in January 1973 with Eagle 265 engine. Then there is one of a fleet of Metal Box 16:Four V8 outfits in 1973 and a 34:Four Bulwark tanker, a model available with Eagle 220 and Roadranger ten-speed, or as the 32:Four in 1971 with 8LXB and eight-speed David Brown.

A new assembly area was built at Oldham, which with improvements at Preston gave the group a forty percent increase in prospective output. Bamber Bridge became the spares headquarters for both factories in July 1971.

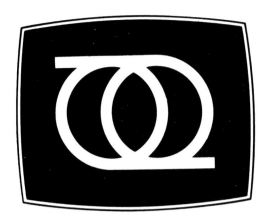

*Photographs this page and overleaf:*
Atkinson's New Zealand plant was sold to the local distributor in 1971 and the South African company was liquidated in 1972 after having built some extremely interesting vehicles. A few South African types are shown here together with a British type carrying an elephant, and an eight-wheeler with African cab. The twin-steer machine dates from 1966 and was the first of this configuration to be built in South Africa. The 6 x 4 tractor dates from 1971 and has a Detroit V8 and Eaton double-reduction axles. It is shown running at 70,000 lbs GTW with a Brockhouse 16 cu. yd. tipping trailer.

Meanwhile at Walton le Dale a new factory was built in 1972/73 with a planned output of 2,500, which took over manufacture of bare chassis from Atherton Brothers Ltd.

*Photographs on these pages and overleaf:*

Seddon's PSV production continued unabated during the downturn in the commercial vehicle market of the early 1970s. A separate Bus and Coach Division was formed at Rhos Works with the transfer of Pennine Coachcraft to an extended factory so that it could concentrate on vans and bodywork. The front engined Pennine 4 with Perkins engines, had sold well in export markets and was made available in Britain. Shown is a 1972 link service Interurban Pennine 6, a model introduced in the previous year with turbocharged T6 Perkins diesel; also the chassis of a Gardner powered Pennine 7 (the first to be available with the 188 bhp HLXB and used in large numbers by the Scottish Bus Group), and the short chassis of a 25 seat Perkins four-cylinder Midibus new in 1972 (also shown in its completed state). A special export model was also produced with Rolls-Royce 209 bhp diesel and from August 1972 Allison automatic transmission could be specified in some models. The bus registered 7608 was a Pennine 5 with 6.354 litre engine which was supplied to Bermuda in the mid 1970s.

In 1973 Bert Dearden, who for eighteen years had been publicity manager at Seddon, died and Frank Whalley of Atkinson took over group responsibilities for PR and advertising.

*Photographs this page and overleaf:*

Before leaving the familiar fibreglass cabbed Atkinsons we see some of the later examples. Late in 1972 their cabs received substantial sound deadening, Syndym rear windows, three-spoke steering wheels and high illuminated roof panel into which the wiper spindles no longer intruded. The unusual sleeper cab eight-wheel van was still in use when more than ten years old. The Borderer was Cummins powered and the Cambro six-wheeler was a dual role machine that worked at 32 or under Special Types Regulations at 60 tons. It had a 240 bhp Gardner diesel and fifteen-speed Roadranger gear-box with two-speed Eaton drive axles to give up to thirty ratios.

*Photographs this page and overleaf, top:*

Since 1971 the Redmonds (Harry was chairman and G. J. and D. W. Redmond Joint Managing Directors in 1973) who were major shareholders in Seddon Diesel Vehicles Ltd. (owners of Seddon and Atkinson) had been holding talks with the International Harvester Company. This large North American truck and agricultural equipment maker had sold trucks in Britain before the War, including 600 in a single year in the late 1930s, and had assembled normal control trucks at Doncaster from 1965 – two 1700 Loadsters are shown. Though these were not a sales success, nearly two thousand had been produced by the time production ended in 1969 with the temporary collapse of the commercial vehicle market. International was keen to break into Europe and in 1972 it acquired a 33 percent interest in DAF Trucks. In January 1974 Seddon, Atkinson and Atherton Brothers were formerly merged into a new firm entitled Seddon Atkinson Vehicles Ltd. employing 2,000 and producing over 4,000 vehicles per year. There were reckoned to be 26,000 Seddons and Atkinsons on the road at the time and the firm held 20 percent of the country's heavy truck market.

This was very attractive to International, especially as the Oldham factory had recently been modernised and given a 520 ft. moving assembly line. Profits had been improved from the £124,000 and £538,000 of 1972/73 back to the record levels of 1971. The Redmonds held nearly 300,000 shares and a 20 percent holding had also been accumulated by the engineering and coachbuilding Cranleigh Group. They accepted International Harvester Co. of Canada's 47.5 pence per share offer in May 1974.

*The following six photographs:*

At the 1974 Amsterdam Show (the homeland of DAF but before the International takeover of Seddon Atkinson) the British firm showed a prototype of its new "European" truck. Experience gained from this and from tens of thousands of miles of testing went into the 400 series, which was shown at London Commercial Vehicle Show that October and launched in April 1975. Assembly took place at the Atkinson factory. Seddon Atkinson's market share in the 28 ton and upwards tractor market had increased from 12.3 percent in August 1974 to 20.4 percent in February 1975 and the firm had invested £3.5 million in the new range. Principal feature was an all-new tilt cab which cost a million pounds to tool, for the newly badged Seddon Atkinson. This cab was of steel construction by Motor Panels, the suppliers of the old Supa-Cab, which continued on some of the lighter models. Some of the styling and detail work was by Ogle. The usual choice of Cummins, Gardner or Rolls-Royce power units was offered in the 400, initially of 183 – 281 bhp. Gearboxes were by David Brown or Fuller and all clutches by Lipe. Axles were built in-house or bought from Eaton.

   The Ellis Greaves low-loader displays the revised badging that came a couple of years later.

Five thousand examples of the 400 series had been built by April 1978. A 16 ton GVW (17 tons where permitted) 200 series had been added in late 1975 powered by the International Harvester German-built 358 cu. ins D-358 134 bhp diesel which revved freely to an unusually high 3,000 rpm and had sufficient torque to work satisfactorily with a five-speed gearbox by Eaton. Perkins engines were available in 14 ton export versions and later standardised when International Harvester pulled out (though not before Seddon axles found their way under International Paystars in Venezuela and Australia). The 200 was effectively a replacement for the 13/16:Four (some versions of which continued as refuse collection chassis and soon captured a quarter of the market) and was built at Oldham at the rate of about twenty per day using a version of the 400's Motor Panels cab. A view inside the Motor Panel's factory is shown in the 1977 advertisement when the 200 won the Truck of the Year Award, as well as an early 200 in service with Western BRS.

# Motor Panels
## the universal cab makers

Seddon Atkinson required a cab that was engineered and styled to match the highest international standards for space, comfort, durability and compliance with EEC legislation.

During the conception of the cab Motor Panels' comprehensive project engineering service and styling consultancy worked closely with the Seddon Atkinson engineers to produce a cab to meet their exacting requirements.

Supporting the production of this new cab is one of Europe's most advanced manufacturing plants, with facilities for styling, design, prototype manufacture, tooling, press shop with complete range of single and double action presses and assembly facilities.

In the fight against corrosion the cabs are processed through one of the most modern automatic seven stage pre-treatment and electrophoretic primer plants in Europe.

Motor Panel's combined expertise and resources have provided a cab which has been acclaimed as outstanding in its class.

## Motor Panels (Coventry) Ltd.

Holbrook Lane, Coventry CV6 4AW. England. Telephone: 0203-85831 Telex: 31367

RUBERY OWEN
RO

Next in the Seddon Atkinson range came the 300 series in 1978. It was a four- or six-wheeler with turbocharged DT-466 International Harvester 466 cu. ins. diesel developing 194 bhp. It had an Eaton bogie and ZF six-speed gearbox.

Harry Redmond had retired in 1978 and David Redmond had moved to International Harvester. That left Geoffrey Redmond as managing director until June 1978 when he resigned and was replaced by American W. N. White. In 1980 International Harvester acquired a 35 percent interest in ENASA, the Spanish maker of Pegaso and Sava vehicles.

Now that International Harvester had interests in DAF, Seddon Atkinson and ENASA one should not forget events in Australia. Indigenous Atkinsons continued to be made there and were ultimately absorbed into the International range. International had been making its ACCO range in Australia since 1961 and before the Atkinson became simply a heavy duty ACCO in the 1980s we show two of the final Australian Atkinsons. The tractor operated by Mecho in 1976 is hauling Wabco dump truck chassis and the "Diamantina King" dates from a year or two later, as does the LP gas tanker.

The 200, 300 and 400 were all progressively updated and became the 201, 301 and 401 with, by popular demand, the big A reinstated on their radiators. The 401, new in 1980, had a less convoluted gear linkage and other improvements and is shown here as an Eagle 340 engined tractive unit as well as in 6 x 4 chassis form. A Perkins powered municipal 2-11 of 1988 is shown as being typical of the vehicles employed by over 250 local authorities. The 2-11 Municipal chassis is used by eleven different specialists and has two or three axles, Perkins Phaser engines and manual or automatic transmission. The lightweight eight-wheel tanker (overleaf) is a 301 with a Cummins LT10 diesel and nine-speed Fuller gearbox. In 1983 ENASA, which had come to know Seddon Atkinson and DAF well whilst all three firms were connected with International Harvester, acquired Seddon Atkinson. International was in financial difficulties and shed many of its commitments in the early 1980s, finally emerging as the successful Navistar Corp in 1986.

*Photographs opposite:*

In the spring of 1987 DAF and ENASA launched their jointly developed Cabtec cab and this was adopted by Seddon Atkinson towards the end of 1988 at the time that Managing Director Gerry Woodhead retired. He was replaced by Vic Wilkes, formerly of Scammell.

Seddon Atkinson had started exporting trucks after a lengthy lapse in 1988 and in the spring was producing 55 vehicles per week, or 37 percent more than in the same period a year beforehand. Great things are anticipated with the new cab, which had already helped Leyland DAF win the Truck Of the Year Award and attracted favourable comment on the Pegaso Troner range. Parts for the cabs are made in Holland, Belgium and Spain and transported in de-humidified van bodies in their unpainted state. The completed and partially trimmed cabs arrive at Seddon-Atkinson from Spain.

A view inside the ergonomically designed Strato cab. A display panel gives visible and audible warnings/information and both the steering wheel and driver's seat are fully adjustable. Initially all models were 4 x 2 and 6 x 2 tractive units with Eaton Twin Splitter gearboxes, Rockwell drive axles and Cummins 200–400 bhp diesels with Perkins Eagles envisaged. The high roof version was known as the Stratocruiser and had two bunks.

Meanwhile the 2–11 and 3–11 ranges were improved and examples of 2–11 seventeen tonner brewery vehicle and diagram of 3–11 tractor are shown here. The 3–11 was also available as an eight-wheel rigid.

**22 L29**: Cummins LTA 10-290

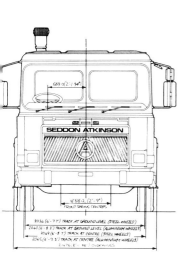

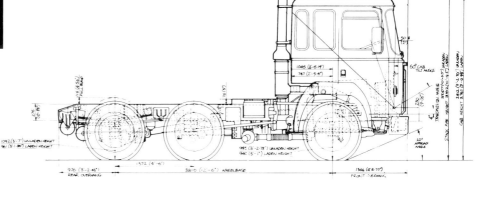

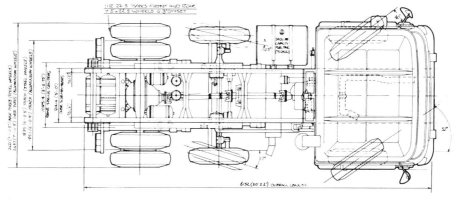

In 1989 the 12 litre and 360 bhp Pegaso Troner was offered by Seddon-Atkinson, primarily for continental operation, where ENASA had built up a spares and servicing network, in addition to the 42 Seddon-Atkinson service dealers also trained to handle the Troner. In many applications the Troner was priced below the Strato to break into major fleets. Here a pair of Troners flank an arch rival—a Volvo F12.

Technical director at Pegaso is Jim Mason, who had formerly worked at Leyland when Vic Wilkes was also employed by part of the same group. Much of Pegaso's background is based on Leyland engineering as the two firms were closely linked in the 1950s to 1970s.

For the foreseeable future the typically continental Troner and typically British 'assembled' Strato will be offered alongside each other, the latter being amongst the lightest of its class. In late 1989 the Pegaso parent company ENASA was acquired jointly by M.A.N. (60%) and Daimler-Benz (20%), with the remaining 20% being held by the Spanish State holding company. Thus, Seddon-Atkinson came under largely German control and who knows what the future may bring?